EUREKA STOCKADE

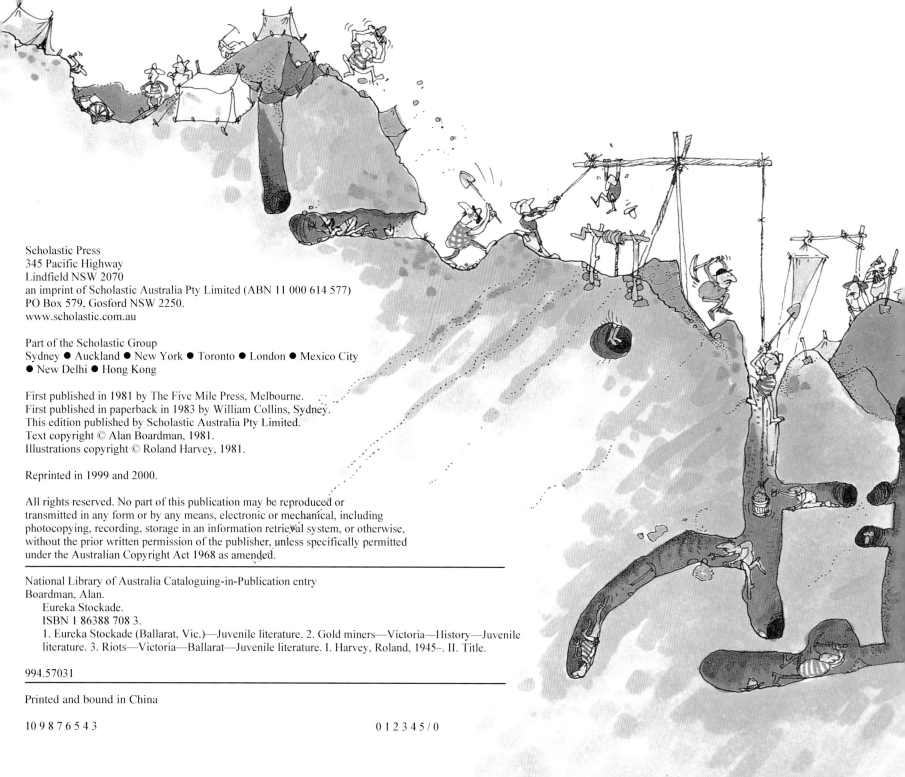

Scholastic Press
345 Pacific Highway
Lindfield NSW 2070
an imprint of Scholastic Australia Pty Limited (ABN 11 000 614 577)
PO Box 579, Gosford NSW 2250.
www.scholastic.com.au

Part of the Scholastic Group
Sydney ● Auckland ● New York ● Toronto ● London ● Mexico City
● New Delhi ● Hong Kong

First published in 1981 by The Five Mile Press, Melbourne.
First published in paperback in 1983 by William Collins, Sydney.
This edition published by Scholastic Australia Pty Limited.
Text copyright © Alan Boardman, 1981.
Illustrations copyright © Roland Harvey, 1981.

Reprinted in 1999 and 2000.

National Library of Australia Cataloguing-in-Publication entry
Boardman, Alan.
    Eureka Stockade.
    ISBN 1 86388 708 3.
    1. Eureka Stockade (Ballarat, Vic.)—Juvenile literature. 2. Gold miners—Victoria—History—Juvenile
    literature. 3. Riots—Victoria—Ballarat—Juvenile literature. I. Harvey, Roland, 1945–. II. Title.

994.57031

Printed and bound in China

10 9 8 7 6 5 4 3   0 1 2 3 4 5/0

EUREKA STOCKADE

ALAN BOARDMAN

illustrated by ROLAND HARVEY

SCHOLASTIC
SYDNEY AUCKLAND NEW YORK TORONTO LONDON

In 1848 gold was discovered in America. In that year, and the one that followed, prospectors from all over the world flocked to California to seek their fortunes in the "Great Gold Rush".

Two years later in sleepy Buninyong near Ballarat, Victoria, another gold rush began.

Until then, the main visitors to Ballarat had been sheep but with the discovery of gold in 1851 people came from everywhere in the hope of finding quick riches.

They came from England, Ireland, Germany, Italy, America and China, as well as all parts of Australia.

Sailors deserted their ships, shopkeepers left their stores and servants ran away from their masters.

They set up their tents and began digging in the hard ground in search of gold. Everyone was equal — gentlemen, labourers, farmers, ex-convicts and sons of noblemen.

The work was hard and many miners gave up after a couple of months and returned home still poor.

Others were luckier and found huge nuggets worth more money
than they'd ever imagined.

By law, Queen Victoria owned all of the land in Australia and the Governor decided that for the privilege of mining and keeping the gold they found, the miners should pay a licence fee of thirty shillings a month.

This licence fee had to be paid by all miners whether they found gold or not and the miners thought it was unfair — especially the unlucky ones.

The Gold Commissioner sent troopers after the miners to make sure they all had licences. This caused a good deal of ill-feeling and often fights broke out between troopers and miners.

In October 1854 a miner named Scobie was murdered near the Eureka Hotel. The diggers felt that the hotel-keeper, Bentley, was guilty of the murder and when the charges against him were dropped they burned down the hotel.

Later at a public meeting on Bakery Hill the miners formed the Ballarat Reform League and sent a deputation to the Governor demanding the right to vote, better conditions and the abolition of licence fees. The Governor refused their demands.

Instead he sent soldiers and mounted police to Ballarat to enforce the law.

The miners responded by building a stockade to separate themselves from the police and troopers. They armed themselves against a possible attack, elected Peter Lalor as their leader and burned their licences.

Inside the stockade the miners raised their new flag, featuring the Southern Cross on a blue background.
   The flag became known as the Eureka Flag.

The soldiers called on the miners to leave the stockade but they refused to do so.

At dawn on Sunday December 3, the troops attacked the stockade and, in the firing that followed, at least 30 miners were killed and 128 taken prisoner. Four soldiers died in the attack.

With the exception of Peter Lalor, who escaped during the fighting,
the leaders of the miners were later tried for treason but the charges

were dismissed by the court and the men allowed to go free.

Following this the monthly licences were dropped and for a fee of £1 a year the miners were given the right to vote and mine for gold.

In 1855 Peter Lalor was elected to the Victorian Parliament, where he represented the interests of the people of Ballarat and brought about many improvements in their conditions.

The men who died at Eureka retain a unique place in Australian history. A monument to their memory now stands at Ballarat.